STEAM MEMORIES: 1950's – 1960's

No. 68: THE BORDER COUNTIES

David Dunn

Copyright Book Law Publications 2013
ISBN 978-1-909625-09-9

INTRODUCTION

This album, the first of a two volume illustrated review of the Border Counties Railway (BCR) in the latter days of its existence, takes us from Newcastle to Reedsmouth. The latter location was of course pure BCR being the junction with the line to Hawick and that to Morpeth and the ECML, via Scotsgap. Although Border Counties Junction near Hexham was the start/end of the BCR in terms of property and former North British influence, Newcastle has been chosen as the start point of our journey simply because the passenger services traversing the Border Counties started from there. So, we venture to Central station in Newcastle and proceed to either of the western bay platforms, 12, 13 or 14, to catch our train to Hawick. En route we will take a brief look at the infrastructure of the North Eastern's Newcastle to Carlisle line which we must traverse as far as Hexham. Just over a mile west of that place we shall leave the NER main line behind as our train veers north-westwards, crossing the infant Tyne over the BCR bridge and begin a magical journey which will eventually bring us to Hawick on the Waverley route. The single track of the BCR begins immediately on branching off the main line and that will then take us through the superb rolling hills and countryside of the North Tyne valley as far as Reedsmouth. Then, in Part 2, taking a longer look at Reedsmouth before moving on westward, still following the course of the North Tyne river, through the Kielder Forest to Riccarton Junction and then to Hawick, our ultimate destination. We shall see stations which were hardly changed from the day they first opened in the late 1850s and early 1860s, their old-world charm still evident even after three changes of ownership! The motive power seen will vary from pre-Grouping types of North British and North Eastern origin, to LNER 'standard' locomotives, and the occasional BR Standard. So, slam the door shut, drop the window on the strap to its maximum opening and sit back in your seat for a long, slow, winding and most enjoyable journey over a long lost bye-way of Britain's railway system: the Border Counties Railway, a jewel to rival any!

David Dunn, Cramlington, June 2013.

Cover Picture – See page 35.

Title Page Picture – D49 No.62747 adds to the damp atmosphere at Reedsmouth on Saturday 13th September 1952 as it heads the morning Newcastle-Hawick service away to the west. *J.W.Armstrong.*

Printed and bound by The Amadeus Press, Cleckheaton, West Yorkshire
First published in the United Kingdom by Book Law Publications, 382 Carlton Hill, Nottingham, NG4 1JA

D49 No.62747 THE PERCY gets the 1627 Newcastle-Hawick train on its way out of platform 13 at Central station on Monday 11th April 1955. Due to arrive in Hawick at 1927 – an exact (but not exacting) three hour journey – this was the last train of the day between the two places; the morning train took seven minutes longer. However, without any delays, one hour and forty minutes of that journey would be spent on the 42-miles of the former Border Counties Railway metals. A nice way to spend a summer evening but you would have to stay the night at some hostelry or other in Hawick (I can think of worse things) and catch the 0615 next morning to be back in Newcastle for 0907. Blaydon shed supplied the motive power as here – but not necessarily one of their own charges – for this working and the engine too would return to Newcastle on that early train next morning. Since LNER days only three passenger trains each way per day plied the BCR between Hexham and Riccarton Junction, with two more running on Saturdays; there was no Sunday service. The unbroken Newcastle–Hawick journey could be made by using only two of the three trains, even on a Saturday, but connections, by changing at Hexham and Riccarton Junction, allowed the Newcastle to Hawick and return journey to be accomplished, although five hours, with waiting time, was not uncommon. Enthusiasts would probably jump at the chance of take the slow train but the travelling public did not because motor buses offered both a more frequent and faster service. *R.H.Leslie.*

When Hawick shed acquired a pair of new BR Standard Cl.2s, Nos.78046 and 78047, in October 1955, they were employed mainly as Riccarton Junction pilots or for banking duties on Whitrope. However, by the spring of 1956 they were working further afield and both managed stints on the Hawick–Newcastle and return passenger services over the BCR. On Saturday 12th May 1956 No.78046 was employed as such and is seen in platform 12 at Newcastle (Central) at the head of the 1110 morning departure to Hawick. The rectangular target board, with 279 neatly painted on, is interesting because it is the Hawick reporting number for banking duties from Newcastleton to Whitrope summit! *H.Forster.*

Standing at platform 14, awaiting eager customers, Blaydon J21 No.65103 has charge of one of the popular 'Garden Special' excursion trains on a summer Sunday afternoon at Newcastle (Central) in August 1955. *R.F.Payne.*

Saturday 13th October 1956 was the final day of passenger services over the BCR. Typically, a fuss was made of the departures, locomotives and the feelings of local people and enthusiasts. Controversy had accompanied the closure proposals since they were announced but a look at the figures concerning traffic receipts would reveal that the BCR line passenger services were losing money – big time! The final day arrived with fanfare and a rush for tickets, most of the five services were comfortably full whereas the 1110 departure was so well booked – it was advertised as a half-day excursion – that six carriages had to be provided as against the normal three (one would usually do). The motive power, Peppercorn K1 No.62022 from Blaydon shed, was ex-works after a major overhaul, therefore in a reasonable external condition because the shed did not expend any energy cleaning the locomotive. Here, shortly before departure, we see the driver posing alongside the wreath of assorted foliage which was attached to the smokebox door. Out of the five departures, only this one, the 1340 departure from Kielder Forest to Hexham with V3 No.67639, and the 2115 Hexham-Kielder Forest, had any kind of memorial offering for the occasion. On arrival at Hexham two more coaches were added to 62022's load making it possibly the heaviest service train seen on the BCR although some excursions and specials had exceeded that number in the few years up to closure (*see* later). *I.Falcus.*

St Margarets based K3 No.61968 had the honour of hauling the last Newcastle–Hawick working, the 1627, and is seen leaving platform 13 with little ceremony and even less cleaning! The usual three-coach load sufficed because there would never be a return working again; Sunday had no services anyway, as normal, and on Monday there would be no services period – abnormal! This train was not however the final passenger service train up the BCR line. That honour fell to the 2115 Hexham–Kielder Forest which also consisted three vehicles, but all well filled because a return was available. The motive power was reported to be Hexham V3 No.67651. Normally, this Saturdays Only service worked back empty stock from Kielder to Hexham but on this special night it was run as an ordinary passenger train, stopping at all stations. Each station greeted the train in their own particular way which varied from the use of detonators, musical instruments. And even a ghost! Now though, we begin our journey embracing time, license, and lure. *H.Forster.*

The first intermediate station, the less than inspiring Elswick, consisted an island platform which though shelter-less in this December 1966 view, had a glazed awning when opened in 1889. The River Tyne is on our left just now but we shall cross and re-cross the river a couple of times before we complete our journey. Once one of the busiest stations on the whole of the Newcastle & Carlisle line, its city location meant that it was up against competition from bus and tram services. The booking office was at the top of the stairs from which the photograph was taken. In 1962 the awning over the platform was taken down but the station had sadly been unstaffed some twelve months before that event took place. The decline for Elswick had started in the 1930s and post-war commuting trends saw passenger numbers plummet further! Elswick closed on 2nd January 1967, just days after this view was recorded for posterity. Demolition and track realignment would make it difficult to trace any remains of the station now. *E.Wilson.*

The eastern aspect of Scotswood's Newcastle & Carlisle (N&C) station on Sunday 14th August 1966: The line here deviates from the fairly straight run from Elswick onto a south-westerly direction prior to crossing the Tyne towards Blaydon. What we see here – besides the rather grim (not helped by the weather) decrepit state of neglect – are the 1880s NER replacement of the original N&C buildings which had been destroyed by fire in October 1879. In the foreground is the top cover of the subway which linked these two platforms and the Newburn line platforms (what a jolly place that must have been on a dark night!) situated to the right and slightly above the spot where the photographer is standing. Parts of this station had their origins back in 1839 but it is difficult to say which, other than the section of the Up platform nearest the camera. A later extension can be made out at the west end of that platform. Fighting a losing battle, flower beds try their best to brighten the place. *C.J.B.Sanderson.*

Standing now on the Down platform of the N&C station on that wet Sunday in August 1966, we look eastwards and catch a glimpse of the Newburn line Down platform waiting shed in the middle distance. The unfenced path linking the two sections of station can be seen rising from the end of the ramp of the Up platform. The waiting shed on the Up platform has been subject to vandalism, the charred remains of a short section of the building lingering on to await the demolition gang. That event would not be long in coming for this section of the station because within a couple of weeks of this scene being recorded, the N&C station was permanently closed on 3rd September during the temporary closure of the Blaydon route. Located just behind the vandalised waiting shed was the goods yard which had been abandoned some sixteen months previously. *C.J.B.Sanderson.*

This is the section of Scotswood station serving the Newburn line. Built much later, and at a slightly higher elevation than its N&C counterpart, which was out of sight to the left of the picture, these platforms were brought into use in July 1875, along with the rest of the passenger stations and goods facilities on the Scotswood to North Wylam Loop. A subway and path connected these platforms to the main station buildings situated on the N&C Down side. Passenger facilities on these particular platforms were just as minimal, with a waiting shed on this the Down side visible whilst a similar edifice, out of shot, served the Up platform. At the western end of this platform can be seen the severed remains of the siding connection into the Scotswood goods yard which closed, like many others on the N&C line, on 26th April 1965; the goods depots on the loop line succumbed somewhat earlier. This part of the station lasted slightly longer than the N&C platforms and closed entirely on 1st May 1967. Demolition followed for the whole station some time later so that nothing now remains. The date of our picture is 14th August 1966 and on the extreme left is a clue as to what we will encounter, especially at this time of the year, whilst en route to Reedsmouth. So, we have the choice of whether to get to Prudhoe along this route via Newburn, or by the N&C route through Blaydon: Tis agreed, we shall do both routes simply because it was once possible to do so. *C.J.B.Sanderson.*

We are on the south bank of the Tyne now and the date is 23rd September 1964, a Wednesday morning judging by the shadows. We are looking upstream in the general direction of our supposed journey which takes a west, north, west, north orientation to our ultimate destination at Hawick on the Waverley route. Why Hawick? Because that was where many of the passenger trains serving the Border Counties line from Newcastle ended their journey rather than the outpost at Riccarton Junction where the BCR actually ended. It will all become clear as we proceed but there is much to see and a few miles to cover. The bridge in the foreground is the road bridge which carried the A695, or was it the A694 which met the former at the south end of the bridge? The rather attractive suspension bridge connected the Blaydon (south) bank with the Scotswood (north) bank from where we have just come. Further upstream and masked somewhat by the road bridge is the railway bridge also known as Scotswood Bridge; its piers can be seen seemingly dangling from the underside of the suspension span. That is our next stop as we take the N&C line first, en route to Prudhoe. One final thought. Tidal at this point, the Tyne has seen industry come and go over the decades of man's industrial history and it might seem amazing now to some readers that when this scene was recorded in 1964, over a dozen coal mines operated within a couple of miles of this spot and, just behind the photographer stood one of the largest coal products plants in the country. Luckily we can't reproduce the odours from that place but more to the point, all of that is now pure history. *Frank Coulton.*

Pampered A3 No.60052 PRINCE PALATINE runs onto the south bank of the Tyne at Blaydon with an enthusiasts' special (1X18) on Saturday 5th June 1965. The six-coach train is still on the Scotswood Bridge which spanned the river diagonally enabling line speeds to be raised on either approach; the Pacific appears to be taking advantage of that fact. We are now in County Durham – for a few miles of our journey anyway – because Tyneside, as an administrative and geographical centre, hadn't been 'invented' yet and T. Dan Smith still reigned supreme! *H.Forster.*

Blaydon shed was just south of the river and it was responsible for the motive working the BCR line so we must have a quick look to see what locomotives are around. Hawick D30 No.62428 THE TALISMAN stables on the shed yard at lunchtime on Friday 16th May 1952 prior to taking on the late afternoon Newcastle–Hawick passenger service. This 4-4-0 had been allocated to Hawick since July 1929 and was to end its days there on 29th December 1958, outliving most of the BCR by a matter of months. Note that the tender has no corporate identity at all, a situation which had been the case since September 1949 when it lost the LNER insignia. Considering that this engine had visited works three times since then, once for a heavy overhaul at Cowlairs, and more recently for a Light repair at Inverurie, it is a wonder that the BR emblem was not applied. Between the date of this photograph and withdrawal, the D30 went to works again on three more occasions so perhaps the emblem was finally applied. *C.J.B.Sanderson.*

Blaydon's coaling facilities had never been modernised and right up to the end, brawn and muscle ensured that tenders were full. This is the coaling stage on Saturday afternoon 26th May 1956 with Peppercorn K1 No.62023 being 'seen to' although little movement or activity around the locomotive could mean that a natural break of sorts is taking place with the disposal crew! The depot closed to steam operations on 16th June 1963, but diesel locomotives continued to stable here until 15th March 1965 when they too were evicted. So what happened to our subject here? No.62023 was delivered new to Blaydon in August 1949 and worked just about every duty the depot was responsible for, including the BCR line. On this day in 1956 the 2-6-0 had just returned from a major overhaul at Doncaster which accounts for its smart-ish outward appearance. It would continue in traffic for a further eleven years, ending its days at Tyne Dock shed before being sold for scrap. *C.J.B.Sanderson.*

(*Opposite*) We are now back in Northumberland, at Wylam, the last station on the N&C before the loop line through Newburn joins the main line on the south bank of the Tyne. This station certainly did have staggered platforms, one either side of the road crossing. In this view, captured on Saturday 12th November 1966, we are looking back in the Blaydon direction where for the final mile the line was seemingly dead straight. Notice the gas lamps still doing their work even at this late date – they did eventually get electricity in these parts – but already that dreaded word rationalisation has been banded around when the goods facility here was abolished eighteen months previously; the severed connection is still in situ. At the time of the photograph, this station, along with all the whole N&C route between here and Blaydon, was temporarily closed (3/9/66 to 1/5/67) but the nearest track, the Up line appears to have had some wheel contact in the last couple of months so something was using the route! Carlisle traffic was diverted over the loop through Newburn until the 'main' line re-opened. The station buildings, signal box, and footbridge are now all 'listed'. *E.Wilson.*

As seen from the train using the Newburn line (Scotswood–North Wylam loop), is the elegant bow-string bridge at North Wylam where it crosses from the north to the south bank of the Tyne, when travelling west. We are actually travelling east in the Up direction, back towards Newcastle but getting photographs travelling in the other direction has proved difficult and I'm sure readers will bare with me. Through the trees can be seen an unidentified 0-6-0 shunting hopper wagons into West Wylam Colliery from the N&C line which is dead ahead. Though undated, this view must have been circa mid-1950s? What was the young lady next to the gradient post up to? *J.W.Armstrong.*

Back on the single route now and the first station we come across is Prudhoe. With the crossing gates closed we have a chance to look back to where we have come from on a wet 14th August (no change there then!) 1966. The station dates from 1835 but the main buildings on the Up platform date from 1880, the small enclosed waiting shelter on the Down platform probably post-dates them. Behind that shelter can be seen a large industrial complex which also hid West Wylam Colliery where, until closure in 1961, more than 500 men were employed producing over a quarter of a million tons of saleable coal a year. Just over half a mile dead ahead stands a large tip of colliery waste which was also half a mile long and hiding the River Tyne from rail passengers, courtesy of West Wylam Col. On the high ground to the right stood Prudhoe castle looking down over the modern man-made landscape. This is the last bit of industry we shall see on our journey from now on as we follow the Tyne up to its source. The roadway we are standing on leads left over the river via a toll bridge to the village of Ovingham on the opposite bank. At an unknown date but certainly adopted by the LNER, the station here was renamed Prudhoe for Ovingham but by 1972 the Ovingham had been dropped. *C.J.B.Sanderson.*

We arrive at Stocksfield station on that same damp day in August 1966. En route from Prudhoe we have passed the site of Mickley station which was opened late by N&C standards in 1859. The place closed prematurely in 1914 when a landslip necessitated slewing the main line onto the land occupied by the Up platform. No such disasters here where the station was amongst the 1835 pioneers, but later upgraded by the NER in the more prosperous times of the 1880s. We are at the east end of the station which, even in the rain, looks attractive and well cared for. By now of course the goods siding has been severed but otherwise the station looks very much like it did when the LNER inherited it. NER features such as the footbridge, offices, waiting sheds and the signal box stand testament to their quality of materials and construction. However, the station buildings on the Up platform are no longer with us, BR seeing fit to reduce the place to an unmanned stop, with shelters. The gardens at this place, which have long been an attraction, still draw the local residents but not to simply admire the blooms and shrubbery but to tend them. *C.J.B.Sanderson.*

This was what Stocksfield station was all about, and still is to an extent although only the residents of the local area drop in now rather than a fair proportion of the population of Newcastle. J21 No.65103 is doing the honours with one of the Garden Specials and it seems the crews themselves actually enjoyed their task, besides conversing with excursionists or simply admiring the flora; remember a lot of footplatemen had allotments themselves, usually lineside too. We have no exact date for this illustration but it would be in August 1955, and may well have been the train seen in platform 14 at Central station earlier on. We can be sure that it was definitely a glorious sunny Sunday afternoon. Simple pleasures and pursuits! *R.F.Payne.*

Stocksfield on Sunday 14th August 1966. Ten years beforehand the flower beds were equally as charming and in full blooming glory whilst the lawns and shrubs were looking just as good. However, the platforms were crowded with interested parties all brought by train from the city. It was part of a day out which took them up the valley of the Tyne to the confluence of the Rivers South Tyne and North Tyne. Afterwards their train would follow the course of the latter river along the Border Counties Railway, stopping at various stations to admire the horticultural skills of the staff. By the late evening the route home took them along the Wansbeck line to Morpeth before heading back to Newcastle. Now, in the year that England won the World Cup, for the first time, fashions trends and tastes were changing and the like of the Garden Specials would never be seen again. Note that electric lighting, for better or worse, has finally come to a station near you. Finally, note that the Down platform is somewhat shorter than the Up platform. *C.J.B.Sanderson.*

Riding Mill station plays host to one of the Garden Specials (No.95) with J21 No.65110 in charge on an unknown Sunday in 1954. Note the staggered platform arrangement with the Down platform located a little further west. The original 1835 station buildings can be seen towards the rear of the train although additions were added during the period before Grouping. The goods yard was operational up to 26th April 1965 when, along with similar facilities at Corbridge, Newburn, Prudhoe, Scotswood, Stocksfield, and Wylam, it was closed. Note the gap in the platform retaining wall, in-line with the tender; this allowed the passage of platform barrows to cross the line to gain access to the Up platform ramp. A moveable, wooden section, of platform was brought into use whenever facility was required. Riding Mill has put on a few flower displays of its own but the leafy surroundings of the station made it attractive to most visitors anyway, especially to those whose daily grind included working in noisy, dusty, red hot or freezing cold conditions and living in back-to-back terraced streets where landscapes such as this were temporary 'escapes'. *K.H.Cockerill.*

(*Opposite*) A normal service train headed by Gateshead V3 No.67688 is seen en route to Hexham with an all-stations stopper on an unrecorded date. The location is just west of Stocksfield, about fourteen miles from Newcastle (Central), with the kind of surrounding to be found in abundance once the BCR bridge is crossed. *J.W.Armstrong.*

Yet another 'Garden Special' makes its slow way towards the BCR. This is No.65103 again but looking quite grotty on this occasion, Sunday 19th August 1956 whilst stopped at Corbridge. It would be interesting to know the itinerary and fares of these trains which appear to have been so popular in post-war Tyneside at weekends. Corbridge was amongst the 1835 built group of stations which survive to this day although changes have taken place in the interim period. The station building – just out of sight on the Up side, beyond the bridge – was granted Grade II 'listed' status mainly for its somewhat unique design compared with other station buildings on this line (they all seemed different anyway). The gantry signal box, seen presiding by the side of the A68 road bridge, was lost to a fire in 1960, whilst the Down side buildings were replaced by bus-stop style waiting shelters; the Up side waiting shelter along with the goods shed were also lost to modern type shelters. *H.Forster.*

The Newcastle bay platform at Hexham on 30th July 1954: Looking west, the main Up and Down platforms are on the left spanned by the tastefully enclosed wrought iron footbridge (I wonder who eventually cleaned those windows?). This bay platform was a later addition to the station – another shorter bay platform was constructed at the west end of the Down platform to cater for BCR services and those from the Allendale branch. *C.J.B.Sanderson.*

Blaydon J21 No.65070 draws up to a BR Mk.1 carriage in the empty stock bay alongside the Newcastle bay platform at Hexham on 29th August 1956. Indeed there was nothing unusual about that everyday occurrence but look closely at the track in front of the engine! Was this a test area for new types of sleeper, reverting back to the earliest days of waggonways, where stone blocks were employed? Note that the pattern appears to be: wooden sleeper, two blocks, sleeper, three blocks, sleeper, two blocks, sleeper! This section of siding track was in fact a relic from a WW2 economy drive to save wood usage. *I.S.Carr.*

Diverted because of floods on the northern section of the East Coast main line, A4 No.60004 WILLIAM WHITELAW runs through Hexham with a King's Cross bound express on Wednesday 29th August 1956. Using the Waverley route to Carlisle, the Pacific brought its formation onto the N&C line with little fuss and bother and here the train has got a fair speed on as it shakes the station momentarily with its 500-odd ton presence. It was the intention of the NBR that the BCR could have been used for such future diversions, and even as an eventual alternative to the ECML; reservation for a two-track layout had been made at all the bridges on the route of the BCR – just in case. *I.S.Carr.*

St Margarets K3 No.61990 waits for the right-away at Hexham on 12th June 1956 whilst heading the 1710 BCR service to Hawick. The photographer will be boarding this train and we can see the results of some of his work later. *I.S.Carr.*

(above) **Heading east away from Hexham station on 10th July 1958, our old friend J21 No.65103 has charge of a goods train it has just brought off the BCR line; within weeks even this daily freight will have ceased to run and the line from Reedsmouth to BCR bridge would be lifted during 1959. The bridge would also be subject to demolition as BR got rid of another headache.** *P.J.Robinson.* *(below)* **Hexham engine shed which supplied so much motive power to the BCR line, along with Blaydon, Hawick and of course Reedsmouth, was closed on 6th April 1959. The two-road shed is seen here at a later date when its rails had been lifted and motor vehicles sheltered inside. Located at the east end of the station on the Down side, the shed had been a sub-shed to Blaydon for much of its life. During the 20th Century it had been destroyed twice by fire, once by accident in 1929 and the other, by design, when the Luftwaffe dropped a lone incendiary on the place in WW2.** *J.Hay.*

B1 No.61330 traverses the crossing from the Down main of the Newcastle–Carlisle line (Border Counties Junction) onto the Border Counties Railway on 21st July 1956. With the River Tyne on the right and the BCR bridge ahead, the train is slowed to 10 m.p.h. Once clear of the bridge a line speed of only 35 m.p.h. was applied for the forty-odd miles to Riccarton Junction. The low line speed had not always existed but from 1951, when serious concerns about receipts and traffic in general were analysed, maintenance of the railway was cut back with a view to eventual closure. Thereafter the slow deterioration of the track bed saw that a general speed limit of 35 m.p.h. was imposed throughout. It was hereabouts where the first sod was ceremoniously cut by the BCR Chairman, W.H.Charlton on 11th December 1855. *I.S.Carr.*

(*Opposite*) At the west end of Hexham station Up platform stood this impressive signal box which had a commanding vista over the whole layout. This view was captured in September 1966, long after the final remnants of BCR trackwork had been lifted but no matter because we can go back in time. Note the gas lamp still illuminating Hexham's Down platform. Such appliances existed at other N&C stations at this time and it was 1972 before it was finally replaced by electric lighting. The signal box too has been replaced although the gantry mounted box at the east end of the station was given 'listed' status and survives. *E.Wilson.*

Different train, different engine, on another day but nevertheless, this illustration reveals that the train has reached the bridge and the start of the single line railway. A closer view of the nearest pier will reveal temporary timber and steel girder structures which were shoring up the 'temporary' girder span which bridged the two masonry spans damaged by floods some eight years previously – the rainfall which caused the floods was reported as 'unprecedented' and fell during the night of Thursday, 12th August 1948. About twenty-one miles from central station now, No.61333 is just crossing the temporary steel span. The cost of carrying out permanent repairs to the bridge, even in 1948, was considered too much for the newly nationalised concern and that certainly was the deciding factor for closing the line. That this end of the route, and the bridge in particular, remained operational for goods traffic until September 1958 seems remarkable, by any standards. *I.S.Carr.*

This view captured from an Up Hawick–Newcastle working, hauled by Haymarket D49 No.62733 NORTHUMBERLAND on 29th August 1956, shows the train leaving the BCR bridge and about to join the main line at Border Counties Junction. The damaged stone parapet was another indication that all was not well with this structure. A section of the temporary steel span – which had already been in situ for eight years – is visible at the bottom of the picture below the photographer. *I.S.Carr.*

Seen from the south bank of the Tyne, a Down train with Blaydon D49 No.62747 THE PERCY at its head, traverses the BCR bridge on a fine summers day in the early 1950s. The river is almost dormant and was certainly hiding the power and ferocity which it could unleash in full flood. *J.W.Armstrong*.

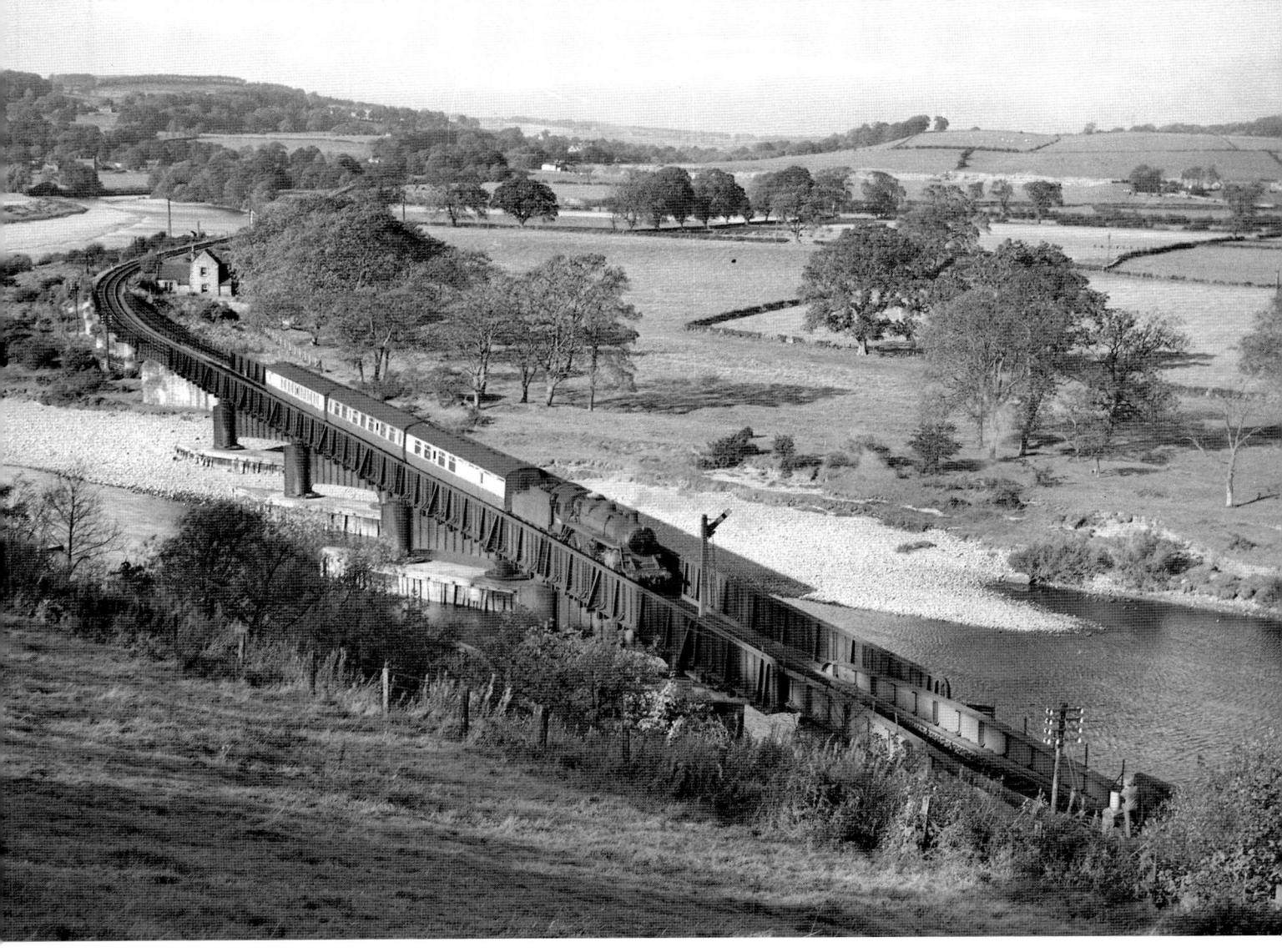

The North Tyne valley; an idyllic scene of which a small part is now long gone. The temporary metal single span bridge which joined what remained of the original BCR bridge with the south bank of the river, can be clearly seen at the bottom right of this 13th October 1956 illustration. Before the 1948 flood, skewed stone arches stood where the temporary span was located. Just out of camera shot to the left was the confluence of the two rivers which created the Tyne; the North Tyne in the top left meandering round its final bend before flowing to meet the unseen South Tyne. Traversing the 'rickety' bridge with care, BR Standard Cl.3 No.77011 is returning from Riccarton Junction to Newcastle with its three-coach load. Due into Hexham just before midday, the train was now running more than an hour late by this point due to a block failure further up the line. This was of course the last day of BCR passenger services and enthusiasts from far and wide filled most trains to capacity. Besides the speed restriction imposed after the 1948 incident, a weight limit was also assigned to the bridge. *F.W.Hampson.*

The remains of the piers of the BCR bridge as seen from the south bank of the Tyne on 13th December 1963. The so-called cutwaters (seen also to better advantage in the two previous illustrations) were shaped to minimise the abrasive action of the water flow on the foundations, the timber jacket being renewed whenever required! *F.W.Hampson.*

Wall station comes into view as we come round the slight bend after covering the first two miles of the BCR. Named after the hamlet located just a few hundreds yards immediately north of the station, this place was well served to bring tourists and interested parties to the easterly remains of Hadrian's Wall. However, Roman antiquities did not have the same appeal to the people of post-war Britain as they do now so that market never materialised for BR. Wall therefore became the least performing passenger station on the line with a mere 138 tickets issued in 1951. Perhaps the next station along, Humshaugh, which issued more than treble that number, was better situated to the turrets, forts and milecastles of the Wall, being half the distance from the ruins. Our motive power for this part of the trip is D30 No.62425 ELLANGOWAN and the date is sometime in 1954. On the left are the meagre goods facilities and passing loop; the white painted shed with the motor vehicle behind was the weighbridge office but intending customers appear to be in short supply today, a trait which appears to be the norm at Wall during this period of its existence. The weighbridge was installed to serve the mineral wagons coming out from nearby Acomb Colliery which was accessed by a short branch line located on the Up side between BCR junction and Wall; that colliery, which employed about 280 men, was producing up to 94,000 tons of saleable coal a year until it closed in 1952, another significant loss of revenue for the line. *K.H.Cockerill.*

A close-up of Wall station on 5th August 1953 with the fire-ravaged remains of the WW2 calamity on the right! Next in line is the station's temporary office and one-time passenger shelter, followed by the signal box. Just beyond the box is the light coloured shelter for passenger comfort which was provided after the fire. This station was opened on 5th April 1858, the first of the BCR passenger assets to come into use during the 42 mile advance towards Riccarton Junction. The gardens here, and at all the stations towards Reedsmouth, were nicely kept by the staff and the sight of the foliage must have been a pleasant experience for arriving and departing passengers. Having the least number of passengers, and a damaged building, Wall was lined-up for an earlier closure than the other stations on the BCR. The deed took place on the 19th September 1955 as the summer timetable came to an end. The North British Railway apparently spent some money on this line in 1890 by lengthening all the platforms and evidence of that extravagance can be seen here where the extension is constructed – unusually – at a lower level than the original 50-yard long platform. The signal box was provided at the same time because block working was introduced, hence the requirement. *C.J.B.Sanderson.*

Seven months after closure, Wall has really taken on an air of dereliction although the demolition contractors are still on site clearing the weighbridge and some sleepers salvaged from the track lifting. The shell of the fire-damaged block could have been easily repaired by the LNER but they chose not to which leaves you with an assumption that they had long wanted to close this station, and probably the whole line, but had not done so. BR soon realised that the whole undertaking was haemorrhaging money faster than it could be replenished so they took the final but not so painful decision, with the help of a rather wet night in August 1948. Cynical thinking would have seen BR repair such damage so that a further case on expenditure could be put forward for eventual closure! Compare this illustration with the previous one; note that seasonal changes brought about by nature do not help lighten the gloom of death. *C.J.B.Sanderson.*

The erstwhile station formerly known as Wall is seen from its northern aspect on Friday 14th April 1956. Some schools state that this end is the original platform and the higher level section was provided in 1890 along with the stone-built waiting room for passengers and signal box. Just seven months after closure, no time was wasted by British Railways in lifting the passing loop and short siding which graced this place. *C.J.B.Sanderson.*

(above) **Blaydon based J21 No.65090 is waiting with an eleven-coach passenger train at Wall station in 1952.** We are stood in the 'four-foot' of the passing loop which would have just about handled this enormous formation if necessary. How the 0-6-0 was going to cope with about 400-tons of coaching stock up the mainly 1-in-100 northwards ascent is unthinkable but it appears to be about to have a go, although not alone. Where the train originated is unknown but its final destination was Woodburn for the Otterburn ranges – it certainly was not a BCR service train. Note that the first vehicle has a number of heads sticking out of its windows, enthusiast style but in this case they were military. *(below)* **Help is at hand! Heaton's No.65110 is coupled up to 65090 now and together they appear ready to tackle the climb.** Now surely that would have been something to witness first-hand! No.65110 had actually been removed from the train at Hexham whilst No.65090 hauled the formation to Wall alone because of the severe weight restrictions on the BCR bridge. *both J.W.Armstrong.*

Illuminated by the morning sunlight of Saturday 14th April 1956, we enjoy a quiet moment after our arrival at Humshaugh station. Also opened for business in April 1858, this place was known as Chollerford but in order to avoid any discrepancies with the next station up the line – and it seems there was a number during the sixty years period before change – the name was changed to Humshaugh in August 1919! The nearest large settlement, actually called Humshaugh, was located a mile away from the station and, in 1927, some 487 souls resided there, according to the *Railway & Commercial Gazetteer*. The settlement named Chollerford consists a small group of properties and is located at a road junction just a few hundred yards to the north-west on the west bank of the North Tyne. The station also possessed a 2-ton capacity crane which was just off picture to the right. The stone landing seen on the immediate right, with a stack of sleepers, virtually marks the spot where the 1890-built signal box once stood. Just when the box was decommissioned is unknown but it would be safe to assume it was when the track re-arrangement took place to get rid of the passing loop, whenever that was. A couple of ground frames were employed to control the siding points after the demise of the signal box, the daily goods train carrying the necessary keys. Note the number of chimneys and their stature at this station. *C.J.B.Sanderson.*

The view from the Hexham end of the station on that Saturday morning in April 1956: On the left is the horse landing or dock, where the carriages of the 'landed gentry' could be wheeled onto a waiting wagon for onward transit to anywhere in the Kingdom; I wonder how often that was used during Humshaugh station's existence? The 1890 platform extension – note the permanence of the stonework unusually employed – had to cover ground already occupied by the short length of track alongside the goods shed and in doing so the shed was effectively cut-off. However, cross platform handling of goods did take place whenever the necessity arose. Being integral with the roof outline, the original awning had to be kept in situ to avoid any expensive re-roofing. At the other end of the station can be seen the cattle pens and the jib of at least one crane. Besides the siding in view, another siding was located on the other side of the cattle dock and that too had facility for end-on loading (*see* later). Note that the platform edging has alternative rather than continuous white lining. *C.J.B.Sanderson.*

J21 No.65033 works the early morning train to Hexham away from Humshaugh in September 1956. This was the last engine allocated to Reedsmouth shed prior to its closure in 1952. Note the catch points in the horse dock, something not seen very often on model railways depicting this type of line. Also of note are the bee hives on the Up side lawn. In the background the line of trees hide the waters of the North Tyne which, in August 1948, may well have threatened this little station with inundation! It is nice to report that our locomotive subject was one of those chosen for preservation. *J.W.Armstrong.*

With the road bridge at Humshaugh framing our view on 14th August 1955, we are looking south, the way we have come from Wall. The ground frame controlled the siding to the horse landing seen previously. Beneath the bridge on the Up side can be seen a, by now, derelict coach which was being slowly overgrown by surrounding foliage. *F.W.Hampson.*

The derelict coach close-up! This magnificent piece of former East Coast Joint Stock was in fact bogie clerestory No.2874, the number still faintly visible beyond the door. Colonel Porter, the owner of the coach, worked for the Ministry of Transport as Inspector of Railway (Big Wheel). On his retirement he was allowed to place the coach body next to the BCR for his personal use! It was located at Humshaugh as it was within easy reach of the Colonel's home at Corbridge. What ever happened to this vehicle in the era when preservation was in its infancy, née conception? Did it become a pig sty, cricket pavilion, tool shed, or simply a pile of fire wood? *F.W.Hampson.*

The view northwards from the cattle dock at Humshaugh with the valley floor to our left and the high ground rising to our right, 14th August 1955. The same geographical contours remained with the BCR line all the way to Reedsmouth. A lone bogie well wagon, possibly of military origin, is stabled in the siding to our right. Such vehicles were not strangers to the BCR and adjoining Wansbeck line. The dead-end siding where the likes of this wagon were used to load wheeled (or tracked) vehicles can be seen trailing off the 'main line' behind the livestock fences. *F.W.Hampson.*

Here is our train for the next leg of our northbound journey. It is supposedly early spring in 1953 as J21 No.65103 approaches the stop at Humshaugh but the 0-6-0 was allocated to Darlington at that time, not transferring to Blaydon until October 1954! Is that an intending passenger on the platform with his suitcase or, more likely, a cabin trunk. The one-coach train was about all the line could handle during winter months. Note that it is a refurbished Gresley Brake in the so-called blood and custard livery. Note also the formally laid-out stones occupying the ground where the passing loop and another looped siding were once situated. When exactly those two sets of rails were retired and lifted is unknown but the garden layout is reminiscent of many created to celebrate the Queen's Coronation in 1953. *D.Dunn coll.*

Just south of Chollerton station was a twin-arch viaduct which carried the railway over the lane to Chollerton village and the station. The other arch spanned a burn which fed the meandering River North Tyne. On an unknown date in 1953, Hawick based D30 No.62435 NORNA crossed with a midday Newcastle-Hawick passenger service which was scheduled to arrive in Hawick at about twenty minutes past two. Like much of the BCR's infrastructure, this viaduct survives to this day. *D.Dunn coll.*

Just one and a quarter miles after departing from Humshaugh, we arrive at Chollerton. The date is 14th April 1956 and luckily it is early spring when most of the deciduous trees have yet to come into leaf, so sunlight abounds yet, at the same time, the feeling of being on the edge of a forest is not far away. This was the first of the December 1859 station openings and the facilities here included goods, and coal siding just south of the Down side passenger station. Part of the original platform is visible on the right with the station building comprising the twin single-storey pavilion type structures joined by the central wooden screen enclosed veranda. The original platform was given over to the goods department during the period when the NBR ran the line. The replacement platform was located just to the north of the cottage, and comprised a simple waiting shelter. Chollerton was one of the highlights on the route of the 'Garden Specials' but to really appreciate the charm of the place you had to stand on the Down side embankment at the north end (*see* later). *C.J.B.Sanderson.*

Chollerton. Again from the south, but a few years beforehand, on Wednesday 5th August 1953: The same photographer had 'snapped' a similar view to the previous illustration, this time recording station staff trying, and obviously succeeding, to keep the growing season in check; no doubt a full time job at this place but easily attainable between the six weekday passenger trains which frequented this station – Saturdays were a little busier with nine stopping trains! Nearer the camera is the goods landing, thought to be the original passenger platform, which appears to be of stone construction with some later concrete additions. *C.J.B.Sanderson.*

On 21st July 1956 Ivatt Cl.4 No.43056 slows for the Chollerton stop as it brings a Hawick–Newcastle passenger working towards the final leg of its journey. Even though closure to passenger traffic was imminent, the gardens and grassed areas were still attended to. *I.S.Carr.*

Chollerton on 5th August 1953 from the northern aspect: The later built (circa 1890) passenger platform might see a couple of customers a day at busy periods! Generally the whole place seemed to be in a state of hibernation waiting for the inevitable. On 15th October 1956 the inevitable took place but other than the failure of passenger trains to run, Chollerton basically carried on, business as usual, although staff redundancies meant that nobody would again tend the shrubbery, grass and flower beds. Today the platform, along with its wooden shelter survives. The station buildings have become residential properties and the little hamlet behind the trees on the left remains much as it was before the railway arrived in 1859 – quiet and sleepy. *C.J.B.Sanderson.*

A close-up of the Ladies Waiting Room and other passenger orientated facilities which were housed in this block located away from the platform. The North Eastern station building at Prudhoe bares a striking resemblance. A glimpse through the windows reveals a scene resembling a greenhouse! Woe betides anyone with botanophobia entering this place. The time is 1040 on Saturday 13th October 1956 and the photographer is patiently awaiting the 1054 arrival from Hexham, the third passenger train of the day to stop at this station. A local man, who may well have been the Station Master and his four-legged companion have come down to the station to see what all the fuss is about. This place was pure 'Oh! Mr Porter' without the mess! Note the war memorial in the station square reminding us that even the smallest of communities sacrificed their young men during the two great conflicts of the 20th Century. *F.W.Hampson.*

Hexham based V1 No.67639, recently ex works and therefore having a reasonable appearance though not especially cleaned for the occasion, runs into the Chollerton platform on one of the 'last day' passenger workings in October 1956, the three-coach 1039 all stations, except Barrasford, stopping train from Hexham to Kielder Forest (arrive 1205). This Saturdays Only working would form the return 1340 all stations from Kielder Forest to Hexham (arrive 1503). Outwards this train was allowed a seven minute stop at Reedsmouth but only four minutes on the inward journey when it did stop at Barrasford. Another SO Down working, the 2115 Hexham to Kielder Forest, stopped at neither Humshaugh nor Chollerton. After its 2241 arrival at its destination, it returned to Hexham as empty stock; except on that final day when, with newly converted V3 No.67651 in charge, it ran as an ordinary passenger train, stopping at all stations en route. Inevitably the grass on the embankment opposite the platform has had the recent attention of a mower for this momentous day in the life of the line. *F.W.Hampson.*

Probably the prettiest of the BCR stations, at least on 14th April 1956, Chollerton had a surreal aura about the place as though passengers would be something of a nuisance in any numbers – less than one a day was enough although the dog might have been happier to have seen more. Amongst the intermediate stations, except for Wall, which was closed by now anyway, this station had the lowest number of issued ticket sales but the greatest number of blooms. Was this one of the reasons for the Garden Specials which ran through here during the summer – you bet it was. Next stop Barrasford and another, though less spectacular, botanic treat. No wonder those Garden Specials were so popular to the people from industrial Tyneside. *C.J.B.Sanderson.*

Barrasford. Apparently this station opened during June 1860 rather than the first day of December 1859 when the line through here was opened. The place was virtually unchanged on Saturday 14th April 1956 except for the platform extension at this south end which had been provided by the NBR around 1890. Note the nearest platform seat which is different from the two original NBR seats in that the metal legs are formed from what appears to be a snake design – of NER origin! Rural the station might have been it already had electric lighting unlike many urban stations at this period. However, gas lighting was probably never employed here because of the remote nature of the place, where gas mains never did, and probably still don't exist. Oil lamps would have done the job prior to electricity reaching the community. There was once a signal box here located on the Down side, on other side of the vehicle crossing, but now a couple of ground frames, one at each end of the sidings, did the job admirably. The rail vehicles in the left hand siding in the distance are in fact cattle wagons which, in the absence of a cattle dock at this station, must have been stored ready for moving up to Wark station. *C.J.B.Sanderson.*

On a damp Wednesday 12th September 1956 a grotty looking St Margarets based K3, No.61990, stands waiting at the head of a Hawick bound working as an intending passenger treads a well worn path towards the ticket hall. Of all the intermediate stations between Hexham and Reedsmouth, this station probably had the best patronage although the 730-odd tickets issued during 1951 equated to just two a day in that particular year! Shortly after the line was closed to passenger traffic in the October, the K3 entered Cowlairs for a major overhaul which was to give it a further four years operational life. *I.S.Carr.*

The appropriately named D49 No.62733 NORTHUMBERLAND, of Haymarket shed, runs into Barrasford with an afternoon 3-coach passenger working from Hawick to Newcastle – probably the 1622 – on Tuesday 29th August 1956. Note the goods crane neatly stowed awaiting its next lift. Did that ever take place I wonder? During the period from 1950 to 1953 the daily pick-up goods from Hexham dropped off a Conflat container which was loaded with bread for the nearby sanatorium. Evidence of quarrying can be seen on the hillside beyond; that may well have been the source of the traffic using Gunnerton sidings, listed in the *Railway Clearing House* handbook, but until 1920 a sawmill was located there. *I.S.Carr.*

Barrasford station in happier times: Wednesday afternoon 5th August 1953 to be exact – with flowers in bloom and creepers giving some colour to the stonework. With only half a dozen passenger trains, and a couple of goods workings, a day disturbing the peace, it enabled the staff to indulge in horticultural pursuits. Of course the Station Master here probably did everything, including changing the points and the bulbs. The two advertisement boards each side of the nearest window were trying to encourage locals to visit Cromer Beach or Yarmouth both of which were former LNER served places just like Barrasford, but during that period of modern history they were still a 'million miles away' and a whole day's travelling from rural Northumberland. Perhaps posters for Whitley Bay or South Shields might have enticed more of the local populous onto the trains on this route. *C.J.B.Sanderson.*

Looking south, we have a last look at Barrasford station on that afternoon of Saturday 14th April 1956. The simple, neat but solid architecture stands testament to the builders of the line nearly one hundred years previously. Goods facilities at this station comprised only the two sidings seen here and in previous views, besides the aforementioned hand crane. *C.J.B.Sanderson.*

This is Wark station viewed from the north-east end of the deserted cattle dock. The date is Saturday 13th October 1956 – the last day, for train working anyway. This place was opened in April 1860, more than four months after the line was opened from Chollerford. Again, the substantial stone construction gives an air of permanence as a dwelling, but not necessarily as a passenger station! Everything was neat and tidy with none of the scruffy appearance often seen at urban stations about to close their doors for the last time. Flower beds have been tended, the platform trolley placed where the brake van of the next train will stop, and four or five milk churns, wait to be taken away on the next working. Towards the south end of the platform can be seen the bump created by the platform extension added by the NBR sixty-odd years beforehand. According to the RCH *Hand Book of Railway Stations,* **Wark station was equipped to handle passengers, parcels traffic, horseboxes, prize cattle, livestock and general goods, a one-ton capacity goods crane being available for the latter. Just a bit further south, in the Barrasford direction, another location known as Gunnerton sidings was equipped with a 2-ton 15-cwts. capacity crane; no doubt a remnant from the days when large chunks of timber were handled there.** *F.W.Hampson.*

A few months earlier on 21st May 1956 the cattle dock at Wark was in business. The station appears unchanged from the previous illustration although a wheelbarrow stands where the platform trolley stood; the aforementioned appliance is further down the platform but is still strategically placed. The wheelbarrow incidentally was also purposely placed so that it was level with the cab of the next stationary locomotive to enable the fireman to fill the barrow with coal from the tender for the station grates. Hopefully a substantial reserve would be available at the station for the winter months in case trains were 'stopped' due to snow drifts and the like. The single storey building on the right was the goods shed which besides being not nearly as imposing as the station building, having a mixture of brick and stone in its construction, was apparently disused by this date. The adjacent platform catered for any horse or 'prize cattle' traffic during the years when such movements were commonplace, especially at rural locations such as Wark. *C.J.B.Sanderson.*

K1 No.62022 and its heavy eight-coach train of 13th October 1956 reach Wark. Even the extended platform could not handle this lot in one go and so drawing up was necessary, making the already late running 1110 from Newcastle to Hawick even later! The K1 and its eight carriage load formed the 1632 return from Hawick arriving in Newcastle at two minutes past eight. If they changed at Hexham on arrival there, they could catch a service which apparently gave them a forty-one minute earlier arrival in Central station! Note the cattle dock is now bereft of any traffic, its loading gauge patiently waiting in vain for any traffic which might materialise during the next two years. Wark presented a substantial track layout and facilities compared with most rural outposts; no wonder a signal box was necessary. *F.W.Hampson.*

Looking north from the south end of the passenger platform, 21st May 1956: The NBR-provided 'hump' is clearly visible from this end but it makes you wonder why such expense, from a Scottish company, was incurred especially when twenty-odd years of operating the BCR had already revealed a misplaced optimism in the line from the start. Nevertheless, the platform was useful on the last day when longer than normal and much better patronised trains stopped here whilst traversing the route for the final time. *C.J.B.Sanderson.*

Another 1956 passenger working at Wark! Headed by St Margarets K3 No.61879, this one is a five-vehicle combination of very assorted stock making up a Hawick–Newcastle train on the evening of Monday 14th August 1956 – just two months away from closure. A lone milk churn appears to be the only intending customer – now what would Dr. Beeching make of that!? A former Reedsmouth engineman revealed that the station stops in BR days did not always generate passenger movement, neither on or off, and sometimes only a batch of *Evening Chronicle* newspapers were the only revenue earners! Reportedly just 504 tickets were issued here during the whole of 1951. Goods vans have now replaced the livestock wagons at the cattle dock, more likely for storage purposes but it was to be another two years before the goods facility was finally withdrawn from most of the intermediate stations between Hexham and Reedsmouth. *I.S.Carr.*

The substantial signal box at Wark on the evening of Monday 21st May 1956: We are looking north towards Reedsmouth, with the North Tyne valley on our left. The settlement known as Wark Common can be seen in the distance. Starting out from Wark on the level, trains soon encountered a 1 in 140 gradient according to the somewhat precarious looking post although that was quire gentle compared to some of the gradients. Nearly three miles distant from this spot was a temporary station known as Countess Park which, from 1st December 1859 to 1st February 1861, was the terminus of the line from Hexham. After the 1861 date Countess Park was no longer used and quietly it passed into history. The photographer is standing on the passing loop which appears to have been used as much as the 'main line' next to the box. The distance signal is pegged to show a train approaching from Reedsmouth – its getting busy again. *C.J.B.Sanderson.*

After 36 miles of running from Newcastle, just fifteen of which were from Hexham, we reach the end of the first part of our journey; this is Reedsmouth in the summer of 1952 – the morning of Tuesday 15th July to be exact. It is worth pointing out that the historical spelling of the name of this place is Redesmouth (as on maps old and new), after the river which flows into the North Tyne at that point, but the NBR with reportedly '... total disregard for any other authority...' changed the spelling to suit themselves! Delving back into railway history it might be a case that a simple spelling mistake by a clerk was inadvertently accepted, and then perpetuated, in various documents so that it stuck thereafter (It would be interesting to see the initial Board-of-Trade documents relating to Reedsmouth). This was the junction for Morpeth, again NBR territory and named the Wansbeck Valley Railway; approximately 14 miles east of Reedsmouth was a place called Scotsgap which became the junction for yet another NBR branch line, the 13–mile long Northumberland Central Railway, terminating at Rothbury and opened 1st November 1870. Absorbed by the NBR in 1863, the 25–mile long Wansbeck line was created, with NB backing (Authorised 8th August 1859), to allow the Scottish company a route into the coalfields of Northumberland via the Blyth & Tyne Railway. An independent undertaking, the B&T had access to most of the coal mines in the area, besides the staiths at Blyth and the Tyne. Although the NBR was physically attached with the B&T at Morpeth, the B&T was eventually absorbed by the NER in 1874, dashing the hopes of the NBR. The period when these Northumberland lines were authorised and built was a period of expansion, great mistrust and even paranoia between the main players: North British, North Eastern, and Caledonian. Interesting times indeed! Reedsmouth's first station, located a little further west of this later junction, was opened for business in 1861 and comprised two low staggered platforms, one serving the passing loop, on the line to Riccarton Junction. The completion of the Wansbeck line afterwards saw the station moved to the junction to create the platforms in this view. The imposing signal box resides over the junction with the line to Riccarton Junction and Hawick (our intended route) branching left, and the Morpeth line going right; a single vehicle awaits motive power in the Morpeth platform. Although passing places existed at other locations on the BCR where goods trains could pass, or even passenger and goods trains could pass, this junction was the only place on the line where passenger trains could be crossed. The station accommodation was situated beneath the large water tank located in the V formed by the platforms. Visible in the distance beneath the footbridge is the coal shelter with a lone wagon, which served the engine shed. *C.J.B.Sanderson.*

Forward to August 1955 now and some evening activity is created by a passenger train in the Morpeth platform at Reedsmouth. The five-coach formation is one of the so-called 'Garden Specials' which we have met previously at various locations en route from Newcastle. Blaydon based J21 No.65103 (again!) runs round its special train prior to heading back to Newcastle with the return working via the Wansbeck line, taking in the Rothbury branch, and Morpeth; a nice interesting 'circuit' indeed. On the initial arrival at Reedsmouth, the special would proceed to Bellingham where the 0-6-0 would run round and haul the train back to Reedsmouth when, upon running through the Hexham platform, the J21 would shunt the carriages into the Morpeth line platform, detach and run forward as here. The passengers of course alighted to enjoy the delights of the junction station and its floral displays. Note that the scale of the signal box is highlighted now by the figures strolling beneath its lofty walls. Visible on the right, stabled in a convenient siding, is a train of artillery pieces which were either en route to or from the Otterburn military training area which was itself located some seven miles due north of Reedsmouth, the nearest railhead. *R.F.Payne.*

Viewed from a train in the Morpeth platform on an unknown but quite late date (note the O missing from the name board), the passenger facilities at Reedsmouth were housed in the rooms beneath this water tank which contained in excess of 60,000 gallons, fed from a nearby stream. Apparently, some years after the line finally closed in 1963, the tank was removed but the stone building was tastefully refurbished for residential use. A similar fate overtook the signal box and both 'structures', including the BCR platform, create a nice setting which would be recognisable by any enthusiast visiting the area. *E. Wilson.*

Saturday 22nd September 1956: The North Tyne and Redesdale Agricultural Show, also known as Bellingham Show day, created a rather busy day at Reedsmouth with three Up trains ready for departure headed by J21s Nos.65110, 65061 and J39 No.64814. *I.S.Carr.*

A quick look at the Reedsmouth engine shed as it was on Sunday 4th September 1949 reveals the tender of ex-LNER J36 No.65331, the former NBR 0-6-0 being identified by its tender cab. Situated on the north side of the Riccarton Junction line, west of the station, the shed was opened on 1st July 1862. Brick built from the start, the shed was later doubled in length westwards and the most northerly of the two roads was extended through the rear wall. This view reveals the shed in its original condition with later added sliding doors covering the arched entrances. On the right is the coaling shelter which covered the wagons from where a lone coalman threw coal into waiting tenders. Note that the wagon road was slightly elevated to give the coalman, often helped by the cleaner/fireman, half a chance to get shovelfuls into the tenders. In 1923 this shed had an allocation which comprised a 4-4-0 tank engine and four 0-6-0 tender engines, all ex-NBR as listed below. Latterly the allocation was more cosmopolitan with a North Eastern flavour; a table below reveals the locomotives which were allocated to Reedsmouth over the years from Grouping to closure. The sleeper-built and earth filled 'buffer stops' appear ready for replacement but that event would not take place because the little engine shed was closed at the end of the summer timetable and the end of passenger operations on the Wansbeck line, finally closing its sliding doors on Monday 15th September 1952. Only one engine was allocated at closure, a J21 and it was transferred to South Blyth on the day beforehand. Motive power was supplied by the NBR initially and up to about 1929 the shed had a distinctive Scottish flavour but from thereon the LNER decided to mix the classes bringing former NER locomotives into the fold mainly because Reedsmouth was designated a sub shed of Hexham. That situation remained virtually up to closure. The turntable, which remained in use to the end of railway operations in 1963, was located just north of the Wansbeck platform. Far from derelict or useless, Reedsmouth engine shed took on a new life after closure and was taken on by an adjacent farmer for use as a barn. It was apparently used as such some forty years after BR had vacated it. *K.H.Cockerill.*

The following list reveals the classes and engines allocated to Reedsmouth from Grouping to closure. LNER numbers are used throughout.

Class	Nos.	Dates.	Class	Nos.	Dates.
D51	1402	1/1/23–?/1/25; 4/6–22/9/25w.	J21	5119	23/12/51–14/9/51.
F8	1583	31/12/29–2/5/36w.	J21	1813	19/12/30–3/8/33w.
J21	5033	17/11/51–14/9/52.	J33	9024*	1/1/23–16/12/30w.
J21	5042	1/4/51–6/1/52.	J36	9624	1/1/23–27/9/24.
J21	5101	2/10/43–3/4/49; 17/7–23/10/49.	J36	9754	1/1/23–29/9/43.
J21	5105	8/10/48–12/9/51w.	J36	9779	1/1/23–22/4/51.
J21	5111	20/3/49–21/3/51w.	J36	9791	7/10/33–26/4/40; 11/1/41–20/3/49.

Only one of class fitted with carriage heating.

: AND SO ONWARDS TO HAWICK IN PART 2.